Dog
Mindfulness

DOG MINDFULNESS

An Hachette UK Company
www.hachette.co.uk

Summersdale Publishers Ltd
Part of Octopus Publishing Group Limited
Carmelite House
50 Victoria Embankment
LONDON
EC4Y 0DZ
UK

www.summersdale.com

Printed and bound in China

ISBN: 978-1-78783-245-9

Substantial discounts on bulk quantities of Summersdale books are available to corporations, professional associations and other organizations. For details contact general enquiries: telephone: +44 (0) 1243 771107 or email: enquiries@summersdale.com.

Dog Mindfulness

SAVOUR EVERY MOMENT. DO LESS, MORE SLOWLY,
MORE FULLY AND WITH MORE CONCENTRATION.

Dannyboy
and Sam Hart

summersdale

MINDFULNESS STARTS
WITH LEARNING TO LET GO.

THEY SAY YOU SHOULD NOTICE EVERYTHING AS IF YOU WERE SEEING IT FOR THE FIRST TIME – SO WHAT THE HECK IS THIS?!

THIS TOO SHALL PASS.

I WILL BE OPEN TO EVERY
OPPORTUNITY THAT COMES MY WAY.
(ESPECIALLY BONE-SHAPED ONES.)

I WILL ACCEPT OTHERS
FOR WHO THEY ARE.

FIRST I DO THE MEDITATION,
THEN I DO THE THINGS.

TAKE THE OPPORTUNITY
TO SEE LIFE FROM A
DIFFERENT PERSPECTIVE.

TODAY IS A NO-RUSH DAY.

SAVOUR EVERY MOMENT.
DO LESS, MORE SLOWLY,
MORE FULLY AND WITH
MORE CONCENTRATION.

I FLOW FROM A PLACE OF GRACE.

SHAKE OFF YOUR WORRIES.

APPRECIATE THE BREEZE
AND INHALE THE FRESH AIR.

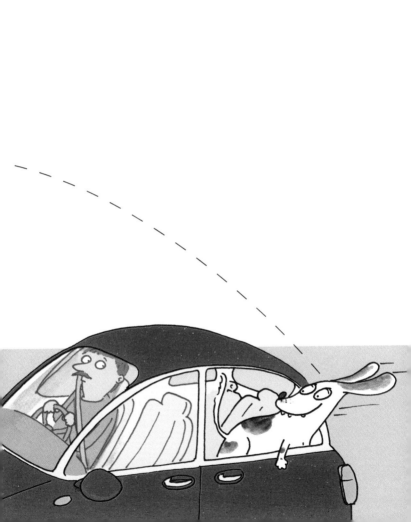

WOW, TUNING IN TO YOUR
SENSES IS WILD.

EARLY MORNING YOGA?
NAMASTE IN BED...

I'M JUST PRACTISING
MY CONSCIOUS BREATHING.

MASTER YOUR DESIRES
AND YOU MASTER THE WORLD.

I WILL LEARN FROM MY MISTAKES
AND GROW FROM THEM.

PATIENCE IS A VIRTUE.

APPARENTLY I SHOULD BE THINKING
LESS AND FEELING MORE, BUT I
DON'T KNOW IF IT'S POSSIBLE TO
FEEL MORE THAN I DO RIGHT NOW.

REMEMBER TO COUNT
YOUR BLESSINGS IN LIFE.

I WILL OPEN MY MIND AND
MY HEART TO NEW FRIENDSHIPS.

INSTRUCTION FOR LIFE:
PAY ATTENTION.

START THE DAY WITH A GOOD
STRETCH TO AWAKEN THE BODY.

FIND JOY IN THE LITTLE THINGS.

MY INTENTION TODAY IS
TO HAVE A NO-SCREEN DAY.

MY BODY IS A TEMPLE.

OBSERVE YOUR THOUGHTS;
OBSERVE YOURSELF.

I HAVE A LONG WAY TO TRAVEL,
BUT WITH EVERY STEP,
I AM NEARING MY GOAL.

IF A THING IS WORTH DOING,
IT'S WORTH TAKING TIME OVER.

I AM STRONG AND CALM,
AND I WILL NOT GIVE
IN TO TEMPTATION.

ALL NATURE IS ONE,
AND I AM AT ONE WITH NATURE.

YOGA MAKES ME SO ZEN.

I AM STILL... I AM TOTALLY
IN THE MOMENT.

FOLLOW THE GUIDANCE
OF THE UNIVERSE AND
TRUST THAT IT WILL
PROVIDE WHAT YOU NEED.

MY WORRIES WILL DRIFT AWAY
LIKE CLOUDS IN THE SKY.

YOU APPRECIATE LIFE SO MUCH
MORE WHEN YOU TAKE THE TIME TO
REALLY NOTICE AND ABSORB THE
AROMAS THAT SURROUND YOU.

I ATTRACT THE LOVE I DESERVE.

WITHIN EACH MOMENT, THERE
ARE INFINITE POSSIBILITIES.

WITH CHANGE COMES OPPORTUNITY.

LEARN WHEN TO STOP,
AND TO APPRECIATE THE
SATISFACTION OF A
JOB WELL DONE.

LET GO OF WHAT
YOU CAN'T CONTROL.

TODAY I WILL SAY "NO" TO STRESS.

I WAKE UP EVERY MORNING,
EXCITED FOR THE DAY AHEAD.

CHOOSE POSITIVE THOUGHTS.

I ACCEPT MYSELF, AND I WILL
ALWAYS BE TRUE TO WHO I AM.

I AM AT PEACE.

If you're interested in finding out more about our books,
find us on Facebook at **Summersdale Publishers**
and follow us on Twitter at **@Summersdale**.

www.summersdale.com